SPACE MYSTERIES

WHY ISN'T PLUTO A PLANET?

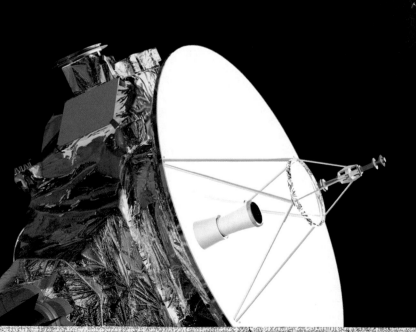

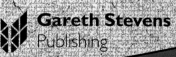
Gareth Stevens
Publishing

BY MICHAEL PORTMAN

Please visit our website, www.garethstevens.com. For a free color catalog of all our high-quality books, call toll free 1-800-542-2595 or fax 1-877-542-2596.

Library of Congress Cataloging-in-Publication Data

Portman, Michael, 1976-
 Why isn't Pluto a planet? / Michael Portman.
     p. cm. — (Space mysteries)
ISBN 978-1-4339-8283-5 (pbk.)
ISBN 978-1-4339-8284-2 (6-pack)
ISBN 978-1-4339-8282-8 (library binding)
1. Pluto (Dwarf planet)—Juvenile literature. 2. Planets—Juvenile literature. I. Title. II. Series: Portman, Michael, 1976- Space mysteries.
 QB701.P67 2013
 523.49'22—dc23

                              2012031421

First Edition

Published in 2013 by
Gareth Stevens Publishing
111 East 14th Street, Suite 349
New York, NY 10003

Copyright © 2013 Gareth Stevens Publishing

Designer: Katelyn E. Reynolds
Editor: Therese Shea

Photo credits: Cover, pp. 1, 29 Johns Hopkins University Applied Physics Laboratory/Southwest Research Insitute (JHUAPL/SwRI); cover, pp. 1, 3–32 (background texture) David M. Schrader/Shutterstock.com; pp. 3–32 (fun fact graphic) © iStockphoto.com/spxChrome; p. 5 martiin || fluidworkshop/Shutterstock.com; p. 7 Science Source/Photo Researchers/Getty Images; p. 9 NASA/ESA/STScl; pp. 11, 23 StockTrek Images/Getty Images; p. 13 NASA; p. 15 Hemera/Thinkstock.com; p. 17 Lunar Planetary Institute; p. 19 Stan Honda/AFP/Getty Images; p. 21 NASA/ESA and A. Field (Space Telescope Science Institute); p. 25 Michal Cizek/AFP/Getty Images; p. 27 NASA, ESA, Mark Showalter (SETI Institute).

Printed in the United States of America

CPSIA compliance information: Batch #CW13GS: For further information contact Gareth Stevens, New York, New York at 1-800-542-2595.

CONTENTS

Words in the glossary appear in **bold** type the first time they are used in the text.

NINE MINUS ONE

From 1930 to 2006, students were taught that there are nine planets in our **solar system**. Mercury, Venus, Earth, and Mars are the small, rocky planets closest to the sun. Farther out are the gas giants Jupiter, Saturn, Uranus, and Neptune. Beyond Neptune is the tiny, icy world of Pluto. Pluto *was* our ninth planet.

But one day, we were told that Pluto isn't a planet. There are only eight planets in our solar system. What happened? Why isn't Pluto a planet? Read on to find out!

OUT OF THIS WORLD!
Uranus, Neptune, and Pluto were discovered with **telescopes**.

MERCURY

VENUS

EARTH

MARS

JUPITER

SATURN

URANUS

NEPTUNE

PLUTO

PLANET X

In the early 1900s, most **astronomers** believed that Neptune was the eighth and final planet in our solar system. A few disagreed. They thought there was a ninth planet. They believed that another planet was causing the **orbits** of Uranus and Neptune to change very slightly. An American astronomer named Percival Lowell used the name "Planet X" for this mysterious planet.

In 1930, astronomer Clyde Tombaugh made a discovery while working at Percival Lowell's **observatory**. He discovered Planet X!

OUT OF THIS WORLD!

An 11-year-old British girl suggested that the new planet be named after the Roman god of the underworld, Pluto.

1930. MARCH. 2 D. 4 H. 56 M.

The arrows point out Pluto as seen from Percival Lowell's observatory in 1930.

7

ICE WORLD

Pluto is a long way from Earth. This makes it very hard to study. One of the best telescopes ever made is the Hubble Space Telescope. It has greatly improved our knowledge of Pluto. However, Pluto is so far away that even the best images of it are still blurry.

Pluto is over 3.6 billion miles (5.8 billion km) from the sun. Since it's so far from the sun, Pluto is one of the coldest places in the solar system. **Temperatures** can fall to –387°F (–233°C)!

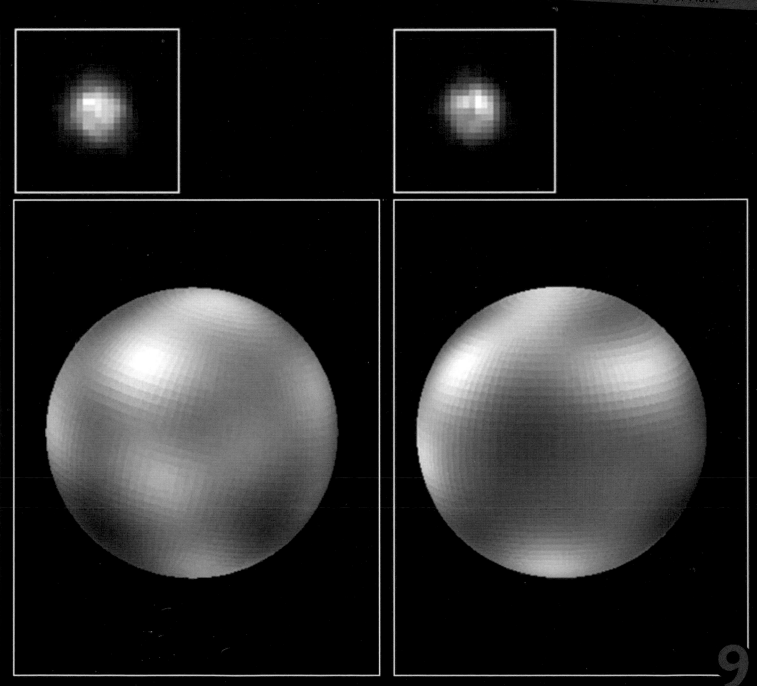

Pictures from the Hubble Space Telescope showed that Pluto's surface has dark and light areas. The top photos are actual images of Pluto.

9

MEASURING PLUTO

For many years, astronomers weren't able to measure Pluto's **mass**. In 1978, Pluto's largest moon, Charon, was discovered. Astronomers were able to compare the two objects to find out Pluto's mass. Until then, people thought Pluto was much bigger.

Astronomers now realize that the discovery of Pluto was a lucky accident. Scientists had been incorrect about Neptune's mass and therefore hadn't figured out its and Uranus's orbits correctly. Percival Lowell's Planet X never existed.

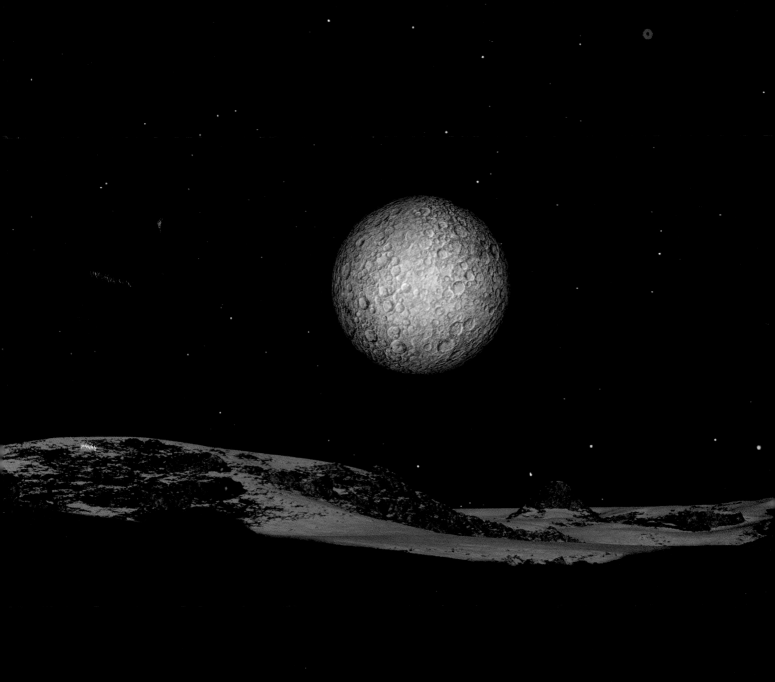

Even if there had been a planet affecting Uranus's and Neptune's orbits, Pluto is much too small to be responsible. This is an artist's idea of what Charon looks like from Pluto's surface.

TINY WORLD

Pluto is very small. In fact, it's smaller than our moon! Pluto's **diameter** is about 1,500 miles (2,400 km). The smallest planet, Mercury, has a diameter of 3,032 miles (4,880 km).

Pluto has five moons that we know of: Charon, Hydra, Nix, P4, and P5. P4 and P5 haven't been given proper names yet. Pluto's largest moon, Charon, is about half the size of Pluto. Pluto and Charon are only about 12,200 miles (19,630 km) apart.

OUT OF THIS WORLD!

Because Pluto is so small, it has very little **gravity**. A person who weighs 100 pounds (45 kg) on Earth would only weigh 7 pounds (3 kg) on Pluto.

Earth

Earth's moon

Pluto

Charon

Though they're really far apart, this picture shows Earth and its moon near Pluto and Charon so that you can get a sense of their size.

13

THAT'S ODD

All planets and moons spin, or rotate, around an imaginary line called an **axis**. Usually, a planet's axis runs from the top to bottom. This means that it rotates like a spinning top. Pluto is different. Pluto rotates on its side.

Days are measured by the amount of time it takes for a planet to make one rotation on its axis. Pluto rotates slowly compared to Earth. It takes Earth 24 hours to make one rotation on its axis. Pluto takes almost 6½ Earth days to make one rotation.

OUT OF THIS WORLD!

The planet Uranus rotates on its side like Pluto does.

This image shows the axis and rotation of Pluto.

THE MISFIT

The planets in our solar system fit neatly into two groups: small rocky planets and gas giants. Pluto doesn't fit into either group. Pluto is made mostly of ice, but probably has a rocky **core**.

Pluto has a very strange orbit. It's not on a flat plane. So Pluto is above the other planets at times and below them at other times. Also, instead of having a circular orbit, Pluto's orbit is shaped like an oval. Sometimes, Pluto's orbit brings it closer to the sun than Neptune is.

OUT OF THIS WORLD!
It takes Pluto 248 Earth years to orbit the sun.

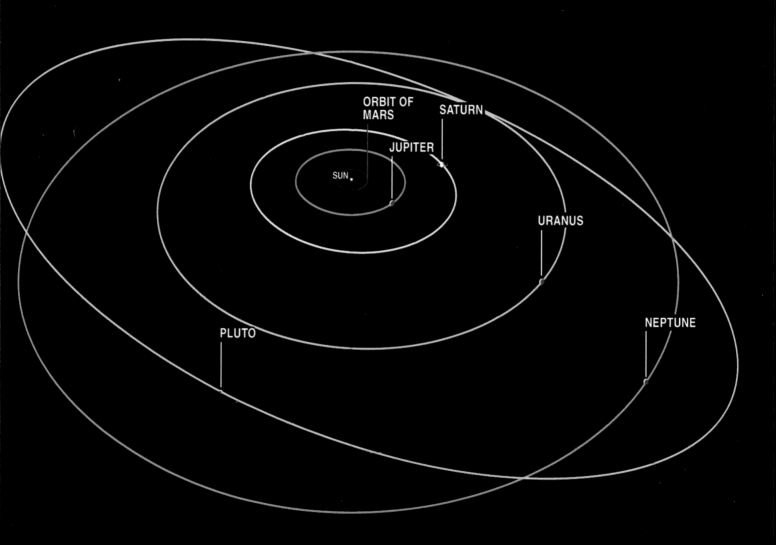

17

WHERE DID PLUTO GO?

In 2001, a newspaper reporter visited New York City's Hayden Planetarium. He happened to overhear a young girl asking where Pluto was in a display of the planets. It wasn't there!

After the *New York Times* published the reporter's story about the missing planet, letters from around the world poured in to the planetarium. The planetarium's director explained that Pluto wasn't included because only the gas giants and rocky planets are shown in the display. People were still upset.

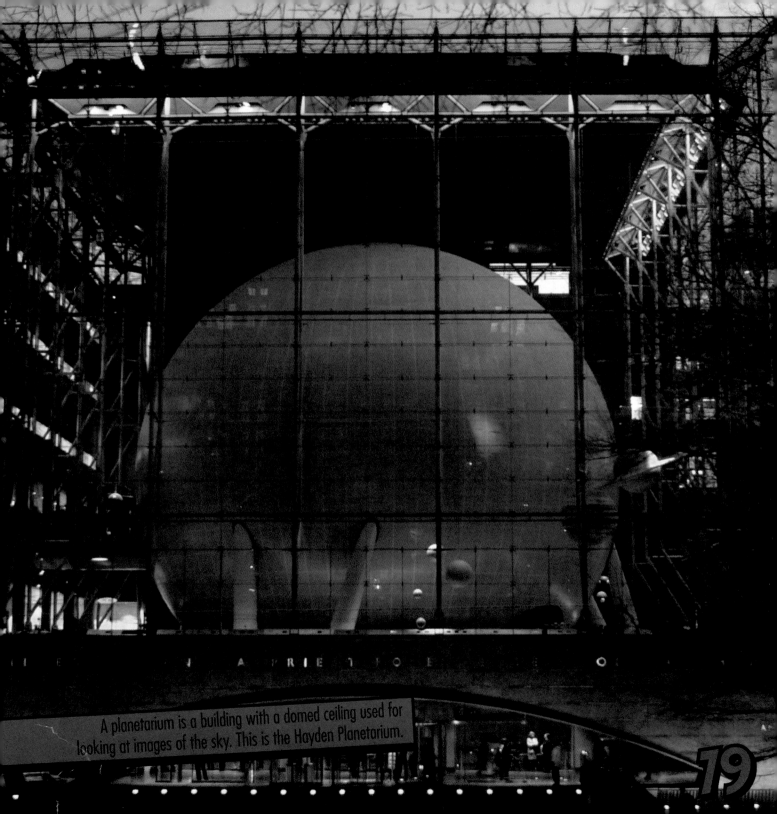

A planetarium is a building with a domed ceiling used for looking at images of the sky. This is the Hayden Planetarium.

PLUTO'S NEIGHBORHOOD

At the time of Pluto's discovery, telescopes weren't as powerful as they are today. There were no space telescopes, either. Astronomers once thought that Pluto was the only object in that part of the solar system.

As telescopes got stronger, astronomers learned there are many objects near Pluto. In fact, there are at least 70,000 objects in Pluto's "neighborhood." Astronomers have named that region the Kuiper Belt. For years, astronomers have been finding larger and larger objects in the Kuiper Belt.

OUT OF THIS WORLD!

The Kuiper Belt is home to thousands of icy objects, such as comets.

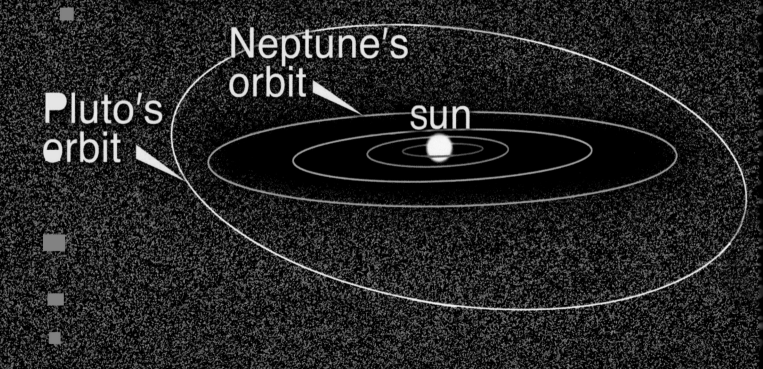

Kuiper
Belt

Neptune's
orbit

Pluto's
orbit

sun

BIG DISCOVERY

In 2003, astronomers found a large object that was even farther away than Pluto. In 2005, they confirmed its existence and thought it was bigger than Pluto. The object, Eris, is believed to be a mix of ice and rock like Pluto.

The discovery of Eris caused a lot of astronomers to question what a planet really is. Was Eris the tenth planet? At the time, there was no clear **definition** of a planet. Astronomers from around the world agreed that a decision had to be made.

OUT OF THIS WORLD!
It takes Eris 557 Earth years to orbit the sun.

Pluto

Eris

Some scientists now think Eris is smaller than Pluto.

TIME TO VOTE

In August 2006, the International Astronomical Union (IAU) held a **conference**. They voted on different definitions of a planet. One possible definition would have given us a lot more planets. Another definition would have kept the number at nine. A third possible definition would reduce the number to eight.

The conference voted for the third definition. The number of planets in our solar system was reduced to eight. Just like that, Pluto was no longer a planet.

Even after the IAU vote, there are still some astronomers who insist that Pluto is a planet.

25

THE DWARF PLANETS

The IAU agreed that in order for an object to be called a planet, it must pass three tests. First, the object must orbit the sun. Next, the object must have become round due to the force of its own gravity. Finally, it must have cleared out all the objects (other than moons) in its path.

Pluto only met the first two parts of the definition. It was too small to clear out all the objects in its neighborhood. Pluto was called something new: a dwarf planet.

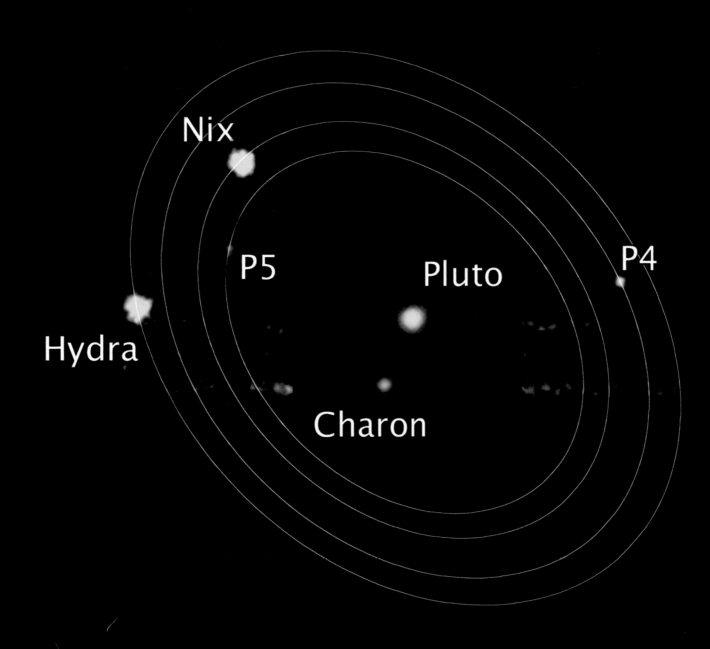

Nix

P5

Pluto

P4

Hydra

Charon

In order to clear its neighborhood, a planet must either draw in other objects or fling them out into space. Pluto can't do either of these.

27

NEW HORIZONS

There is still much we don't know about Pluto. Since its discovery in 1930, Pluto has remained a dark and mysterious world. In 2006, NASA (National Aeronautics and Space Administration) launched a spacecraft made to study Pluto. The *New Horizons* spacecraft will fly past Pluto in 2015.

New Horizons will take the first close-up images of Pluto and its moon Charon. Afterwards, it will move on to study other objects in the Kuiper Belt.

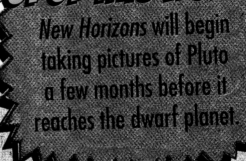

OUT OF THIS WORLD!

New Horizons will begin taking pictures of Pluto a few months before it reaches the dwarf planet.

PLUTO FACTS

length of year	about 248 Earth years
length of day	about 6.4 Earth days
average distance from sun	3.6 billion miles (5.8 billion km)
diameter	1,500 miles (2,400 km)
maximum temperature	−369°F (−223°C)
minimum temperature	−387°F (−233°C)

New Horizons will be close to Pluto for only about 30 minutes.

GLOSSARY

astronomer: a person who studies stars, planets, and other heavenly bodies

axis: an imaginary straight line around which an object turns

conference: a meeting for people with a common interest

core: the central part of something

definition: a short statement explaining what a word or concept means

diameter: the distance from one side of a round object to another through its center

gravity: the force that pulls objects toward the center of a planet, star, or moon

mass: the amount of matter in an object

observatory: a place used for the scientific observation of heavenly bodies

orbit: to travel in a circle or oval around something, or the path used to make that trip

solar system: the sun and all the space objects that orbit it, including the planets and their moons

telescope: a tool that makes faraway objects look bigger and closer

temperature: how hot or cold something is

FOR MORE INFORMATION

BOOKS

Landau, Elaine. *Pluto: From Planet to Dwarf.* New York, NY: Children's Press, 2008.

Metzger, Steve. *Pluto Visits Earth!* New York, NY: Orchard Books, 2012.

Scott, Elaine. *When Is a Planet Not a Planet? The Story of Pluto.* New York, NY: Clarion Books, 2007.

WEBSITES

King of the Ice Dwarfs
spaceplace.nasa.gov/ice-dwarf/
Check out this fun NASA site for more facts about Pluto.

Pluto
www.kidsastronomy.com/pluto.htm
Read facts about Pluto and other space objects.

INDEX